# The Pocket
# Athletic Director

Dick King

**BookPartners**
Wilsonville, Oregon

Publisher's Cataloging-in-Publication
King, Dick, 1933–
  The pocket athletic director / Dick King. —
[Completely revised ed.]
       p.    cm.
1. School sports—United States—Management—
Handbooks, manuals, etc. 2. Sports administration—
United States—Handbooks, manuals, etc. 3.
Athletics—United States—Management —
Handbooks, manuals, etc. I. Title

GV346.K55 1999
371.'18'9—DDC 21        99-72674

ISBN 1-58151-037-3        Cataloging by Shiela K. Oshsroff

Cover design by Richard Ferguson
Text design by Sheryl Mehary

***BookPartners, Inc.***
P. O. Box 922
Wilsonville, Oregon 97071

# Introduction

Athletic Directors, athletic administrators, and coaches are busy people. If they're doing their jobs right, they have dozens of important issues to deal with, every hour of every day, and each issue will probably raise questions about rules and policies. There's so much to know, so much to read, so much to learn! Any AD wants to do the job well, but it's easy to get so caught up in the mundane chores that the reading may not get done.

When ADs make mistakes, it's almost always because:

- they were ignorant of the rules, or
- they misinterpreted the rules, or
- they trusted the wrong people to provide accurate information.

Do not assume that your coaches know and fully understand the policies, rules, and programs. If there have not been regular efforts to reinforce their understanding, it is possible that coaches will begin to interpret and enforce rules as they see fit. This creates a clear danger that enforcement will be arbitrary and capricious, an invitation to legal challenges. Coaches are obligated to enforce and uphold school rules and regulations, and ADs are responsible for making certain that the coaches know and understand these rules.

I wrote this little book with only one purpose: to help ADs and coaches avoid the pitfalls that await the inexperienced athletic administrator. It does not contain everything you need to know, but it does provide, in plain language, descriptions of the aspects of athletic administration that are likely to present challenges to conscientious leaders.

The book consists of a series of topics, arranged in alphabetical order so that you can access a topic quickly once you are familiar with the book. To get you started and help you find topics you don't look up often, there is a "Topic Finder" or index at the beginning of the text.

Especially sensitive areas are signaled by the whistle symbol. Consider these "red alerts" to potential problems and very important knowledge. Ignoring them is like ignoring an official's whistle!

Many of the things a coach or AD has to know are specific to a state, school district, or school. To make this a real handbook for constant reference, we've included fill-in boxes where you can note down the rules, policies, or other information that apply to your program. One way an AD can use this book is to pass out copies during the annual orientation meeting for coaches. Tell the staff what to write in the fill-in boxes; the physical act of writing it down will help fix it in their minds. Alternatively, assign the fill-ins as "homework" to encourage staff members to familiarize themselves with the state association's rule book and other pertinent sources.

I would like to acknowledge those whose contributions made this book possible: Shelly Thiel, athletic director, Enumclaw (Washington) High School; Gene Rostvold, athletic director, Yakima (Washington) Schools; Derald Cox, athletic director, Flagstaff (Arizona) High School; Joe Bullock, athletic director, Tacoma (Washington) High School; and Dick Sauers, principal, Granite Hills (California) High School.

Dick King
Renton, Washington

# Topic Finder

# Awards

*Criteria* for earning a school letter, or any other award, should not be secret documents. Coaches should clearly write out the requirements for earning each award offered in the sports they supervise and make it available for all to read.

*Allowable awards* are generally limited to those given by a school to its own students: letters, insignia, certificates, medals, and trophies. The intrinsic (monetary) value of these awards must be insignificant. This principle also applies to awards from outside sources—for example, "outstanding player" trophies from news media or service clubs, or awards for individual sports such as golf or tennis.

 Beware of the overzealous supporter who wants to present a new television set to the MVP of the championship football team! Check your state association handbook to determine whether there is a rule covering awards from outside the school. Do not assume that just because such an award has been given in the past, it is legal.

---

**Summarize state association policy on allowable outside awards:**

_____

_____

_____

_____

_____

_____

---

# Attendance

Many schools have rules requiring that a student attend a specific number of classes in order to participate in interscholastic activities on a given day. Three classes, or half the day, is a common standard. The chances are pretty decent that some of your coaches don't know (or even know about) this rule. Students are quick to pick up on inconsistent or casual enforcement of rules, so be sure the coaches and the athletes know and follow this one.

**How many classes must an athlete attend on a given day in order to participate in an interscholastic activity on that day?** _____

## Attendance area

This can be a source of confusion. Some school districts that have multiple high schools declare their district "open," and students are permitted (with some restrictions) to attend the school of their choice. The thoughtful AD will become familiar with both local district guidelines and state association rules. This is one of several problem areas that affect eligibility. In this case, students, their parents, or coaches may attempt to abuse the open enrollment option in order to transfer athletes to schools that would not ordinarily accept them.

**Does your district permit high school students to choose their school?**

_____

---

**What state association rules, if any, deal with "open" enrollment?**

_____

_____

_____

_____

_____

_____

_____

---

# Boosters clubs

Coaches who perceive parents of their student-athletes as increasingly contentious may have a tendency to avoid contact with the parents, and this creates a communications gap. Boosters clubs provide a forum in which coaches and administrators can present their plans and the fundamental positions from which the plans were drawn. These organizations also give schools excellent opportunities to educate adults, especially about the aims and objectives of school sports programs. As every coach or AD knows, ignorant and misinformed "fans" are among the worst kinds.

To promote teamwork on the part of the coaching staff, it is vital that all sports have an opportunity to profit from boosters' fundraisers. The AD is responsible for ensuring that "one-sport dynasties" do not develop at the expense of other sports. All sports are integral to the general education plan, and they are definitely not profit-seeking activities for aspiring professional athletes.

Be aware that some of the most popular fundraising activities involve some form of gambling, such as Bingo or "casino nights." In such cases, the boosters club may have to acquire the proper permit.

To avoid becoming a stage for attacking coaches, a boosters club needs a well-crafted constitution. That document should absolutely prohibit the "get the coach" behavior that educators are right to fear.

# Cheerleaders

It is common for schools to establish enhanced eligibility standards for cheerleaders. As AD, you'll want to know the answers to the following questions:

**How are cheerleaders selected?**

_____

_____

_____

_____

**Who makes squad assignments?**

_____

_____

_____

_____

**What GPA must a cheerleader maintain?** _____

**What other constraints are there on cheerleaders' eligibility?**

_____

_____

_____

_____

**Who supervises cheerleaders at "away" contests?**

_____

_____

_____

Transportation of cheerleaders to "away" contests may be provided by the school district, perhaps by a van-driving volunteer. Cheerleaders may ride on the players' buses. In urban areas, cheerleaders often arrange their own transportation to game sites.

# Coaches

Communicating with all the coaches is not an easy job. The athletic department is in a sense the largest department in any secondary school. The coaching staff at a large high school may number as many as forty individuals, and fewer than half of these may be teachers in the school. As a matter of fact, many of them may not be teachers at all.

One good way to communicate with your school's coaches is through a monthly newsletter, distributed by mail to all the coaches. It can feature notices, reminders, new information, and other pertinent topics. Another strategy is to hold monthly breakfast meetings, aimed at in-season coaches but open to all coaches.

If you are the school representative who attends league (conference, division, district, etc.) meetings, do not be satisfied with merely distributing copies of the minutes to your coaches. Because they weren't present for the discussions that took place, the coaches will choose their own contexts as they peruse these bare-bones notes, and they may completely misunderstand the motives of those who did the decision-making. Instead, summarize the important points in your newsletter or meeting presentation and explain how they apply to your particular situation.

The majority of states now require (or strongly recommend) continuing education for coaches. One aim of these programs is to provide in-service training for coaches who are not classroom teachers, but the bottom line is the safety of student-athletes. Schools are obligated to provide safe environments for their school-sponsored activities, and coaches must learn to be conscious agents of the school district in this effort.

---

**What is your state's requirement for continuing education for coaches?**

_____

_____

_____

_____

---

Every AD needs to keep a file with the complete academic record (transcripts) of all the coaches. The file must include clear evidence that all coaches have current First Aid/CPR certification (or the alternative preferred by the district).

Hiring coaches, or otherwise adding personnel to the staff—even volunteers—can be a major headache. Many schools are responding to the challenge by establishing clearly stated criteria. For example, candidates who are teachers at the school may be given preference, as may those who have had extensive training and experience in First Aid/CPR. Letters of reference may also be required. In many states, anyone who works for a school, even part-time or temporarily, must undergo a criminal background check and fingerprinting.

The nation's courts have provided a guideline to how much preparation an individual should have before a school permits him or her to supervise or conduct an activity. As Jerry Pflug and I put it in our 1982 book *The Professionally Responsible Coach,* "A coach must be able to perform as though he/she were completely qualified to instruct the activity." Competence strongly implies the ability to anticipate, which means (at the very least) that the coach

- has adequate knowledge of the rules of the activity;
- is well versed in the techniques and skills required;
- is familiar with the nature of the activity and can therefore anticipate when and where most injuries are likely to occur.

Evaluating coaches is next to impossible unless the AD has three things: a job description, specific evaluation criteria, and a formal approach to observation. Some states have created completely separate, non-continuing contracts for coaches (and certain others), and the law may not require that school officials disclose reasons for not rehiring a coach. Failure to provide an explanation, however, may lead students, teachers, and community members to draw incorrect conclusions. In the absence of official explanation, rumors and ugly exaggerations can arise. At the very least, an AD should be able to refer to an official (adopted by the school board) job description for each coaching position.

**Does your school district have a special type of non-continuing contract for coaches?**

_____

_____

_____

**Do your coaches have written job descriptions approved by the school board?**

_____

_____

_____

_____

Who can coach at your school? A few states require head coaches in certain sports to be certified teachers and to be employed by the school district for which they want to coach. In almost every state, however, there are waiver provisions available. About half the states require special training for all coaches at all levels. A few states mandate competencies to be attained and have developed continuing education programs for both teaching and non-teaching coaches. Your school district undoubtedly has a policy on employing coaches, and you will want to familiarize yourself with that policy before answering questions from or about candidates for coaching vacancies.

---

**Must your coaches be certified teachers?** _____

**Must a coach be currently teaching in the district?** _____

**Can these requirements be waived?**
_____

---

**Does your state require special training for coaches?**

_____

_____

**Must your coaches be certified in First Aid and CPR?**_____

**Does your school district require a criminal background check for coaches?**_____

**Where can you find information about the competency and continuing education requirements mandated by your state? By your school district?**

_____

_____

_____

At least half of all states require current First Aid/CPR certification. Principals or their designees, often ADs, are usually responsible for ensuring that the requirement is satisfied. It would be a foolhardy administrator who, in these litigious days, failed to make this responsibility a top priority.

## Communicating

It has become a relatively common practice to schedule opening-of-season meetings and to invite students, parents, and boosters to meet with coaches to share information. These sessions offer excellent opportunities for presenting the basic goals, objectives, and expectations of the school sports program.

To teachers and other school staff members, ADs represent the best source of reliable information about local school sports programs. Staff should be provided with sports calendars, copies of eligibility requirements, up-to-date information about participation, and copies of newsletters produced by the athletic department.

The media require the assistance of schools to report on the many interscholastic sports contests held. Often head coaches are expected to call in the results to newspaper sports reporters, but there are other options—assistant coaches, for example. Students interested in sportswriting can be trained to take on this important responsibility. There may be someone in the boosters club who has a background in sports journalism and would enjoy doing this.

The AD must be especially quick to alert and inform whenever a serious accident or injury occurs. Those who "need to know" may include parents, school officials, coaches' family members, or others identified by school district policy. Head coaches must be completely familiar with the reporting policy (see "Injuries" below), since the AD will not be present at all contests.

## Conduct

Student-athletes are often asked to meet a higher standard of conduct than that required of other students. Local school districts often have deportment codes, as do most state associations. For example, in many states, expulsion from a contest results in a one-contest suspension from competition. A second expulsion can result in even more severe penalties.

**Give examples of conduct standards required of your student-athletes and the penalties for failing to observe these.**

_____

_____

_____

_____

_____

_____

_____

_____

_____

*conduct*

Many school districts have adopted substance abuse policies, and some have considered testing athletes for drugs. Your school may have a policy that covers all athletes, or a special policy covering just those who represent the school in interscholastic activities. Drug testing of athletes can be legal when it is done according to the guidelines established by the U.S. Supreme Court in *Vernonia SD v. Acton* (1995). (See also the section on "Substance abuse" in this book.)

**Who is covered by your school's substance abuse policy? Is there a separate policy for interscholastic sports participants?**

_____

_____

_____

**Does your school test athletes for drugs?**_____

# Contests

Every state association limits the number of "contests" in which individuals and teams may compete during a given period, and they clearly define what a "contest" is: any event that involves participants from two or more schools. Be especially wary of requests by coaches to enter their teams in "jamborees," "pre-season practice games," or "scrimmages." The various state associations differ on the kinds and numbers of pre-season activities they permit. Check your state association handbook, looking under such headings as "General Sports Rules," "Contest Limitations," or "Rules Governing Contests."

Some states permit jamborees, which are usually abbreviated contests. All state associations have specific rules that create clear separation between jamborees and contests. Typical requirements of a jamboree include:

- More than two schools must be involved.
- Each participating school must play at least two opponents.

### *contests*

- Only students who have met all eligibility requirements may take part.

"Play days" are normally defined as events in which teams and individuals do not represent their schools. Play days are usually associated with physical education programs, not with interscholastic sports.

Beware of overscheduling. In some team sports, participation in "invitationals" is allowed, and the state may allow one or two such tournaments to count as single contests. After the specified number of tourneys, however, any match played must count against the limit.

Contest limitations for individuals are intended to safeguard the health, safety, and well-being of student-athletes by limiting the amount of competition in which an athlete can participate within a given day, week, or season. Violations of these rules may result in forfeiture.

Contest limitations for teams vary from state to state, and the prudent AD will always check schedules against association rules before signing off on them. Contest limitation rules are not hard to find: they ordinarily appear at the beginning of each specific sport section in a state association's handbook.

---

**What kinds of extra-season activities are permitted in your region?**

_____

_____

_____

_____

_____

**What limitations are placed on individuals?**

_____

_____

_____

_____

---

# Dance and drill teams

Not all states regulate school dance and drill teams. Those that do may do no more than set starting (fall) and ending (spring) dates for the activity. Local school districts or individual schools may have established eligibility rules and codes of conduct for members of these performance units, and they may require that supervisors (coaches or sponsors) be present for all public presentations.

New ADs are occasionally surprised to discover (usually as the result of an ugly confrontation) that they are responsible for scheduling halftime programs for (at least) varsity football and basketball contests. At least two weeks before the start of a season, the AD should meet with all those who have an interest in presenting halftimes. Be certain to include coaches in the meeting, since they may be working to develop youth groups who will want opportunities to perform.

> **Does your state association regulate dance and drill teams?**_____
>
> **Does your school have separate eligibility codes and conduct rules for dance and drill team members?**
>
> _____
>
> **In your school, who is responsible for organizing halftime programs?**
>
> _____

## Eligibility

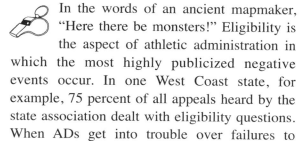

In the words of an ancient mapmaker, "Here there be monsters!" Eligibility is the aspect of athletic administration in which the most highly publicized negative events occur. In one West Coast state, for example, 75 percent of all appeals heard by the state association dealt with eligibility questions. When ADs get into trouble over failures to perform well in this area, it will probably result from:

## *eligibility*

- ignorance of state association, local league, or school district rules; or
- lies told by students or their parents or guardians; or
- failure by the AD to carefully check official transcripts and other school records.

All school officials have an obligation to promote the spirit of rules adopted by the state association to which they belong. They have an obligation to deny to cheaters and liars the benefits they seek to gain through flagrant dishonesty. This means that you will need a resident expert on eligibility, and it is natural that the AD move into this position. Remember that violations of eligibility often result in forfeitures, an eventuality that will surely incur the wrath of students, coaches, parents, staff, superiors, and the local media. No matter what the facts of an individual case may be, the AD is likely to be held culpable for not having dotted all the i's and crossed all the t's. Read the following discussion carefully.

Both your state and your school probably have *academic eligibility standards* for students who wish to participate in sports. States commonly establish minimal requirements of "passing" grades or specific grade point average (GPA). The minimum GPA is usually between 1.7 and 2.1. Local school boards often specify higher minimum standards than those required by the state.

These policies probably specify that a student can continue to compete for a certain period of time (perhaps one or two weeks) after failing to meet the standard. States often detail the steps a student must take to regain eligibility.

Individual coaches often conduct "grade checks" to monitor all their athletes, or those who have a history of poor grades. The AD should determine the degree to which the teaching faculty willingly supports coaches in this monitoring process. Some teachers may resent what they perceive as unproductive extra work and will need to be reassured that they are not wasting their time reporting students' progress to coaches.

Your school district probably has an *appeal process f*or the benefit of students. ADs must be familiar with this process in order to safeguard the rights of students. Be aware that there are always deadlines to meet and proper procedures to follow.

---

**What is your state's required GPA for student athletes?** _____

**If the school's requirement is different, what is it?**

_____

**Do school faculty cooperate with coaches to monitor grades?**

_____

**Does your school have an appeal process for academic eligibility?**

_____

**Where is this process set out?**

_____

---

*Age* is a factor in determining who may compete in school-sponsored sports. ADs should consult their state association handbook to determine what age limits are in effect, and the dates on which age must be checked. For example, a rule might specify that a competitor "must not be 20 by September 1."

---

**What are the minimum and maximum ages at which students may compete in your system?**

_____

**On what date is this age calculated?**

_____

---

 Although university-level athletes have five years (from the date of their enrollment) to use their *four years of eligibility,* this is not true in high school sports! From the time of enrollment in ninth grade, high school students have only four years in which they may compete. However, most state associations allow appeals for exemptions to this rule in "hardship" cases, when a student has been forced by exceptional circumstances to miss participa-

*eligibility*

tion in sports for a period. This kind of exemption is intended to benefit students who have suffered such things as severe illness or family catastrophes, but it is routinely abused by athletic directors who wish to extend the eligibility of students who have lost eligibility through academic failure. Spurious appeals have often resulted in the extension of eligibility, and this is currently a subject of great controversy in West Coast associations at least.

*Enrollment status* is a key to ascertaining eligibility. Some important questions the AD must answer are summarized in the following fill-in boxes. Note that a "previous semester rule" states that in order to compete in the current semester (or trimester), a student must have been regularly attending school in the immediately preceding semester (trimester).

**Must participating students attend your school full time? _____**

**Does the state association or the school district determine whether a student is "full time"?** _____

**How does enrollment in a vocational or other alternative program affect eligibility?**

_____

_____

_____

_____

**Is there a "cut-off date" prior to which a student must be enrolled and in attendance before eligibility is possible?**

_____

**Does your state association have a "previous semester" rule?**

_____

## *eligibility*

*Foreign students* may not be eligible to compete in varsity sports. Do not permit any foreign student to participate in any varsity contest until you have determined that your state association permits students on visas to play in varsity contests. (Sub-varsity contests may be okay, but you must check the rules to ascertain this.)

---

**Does your state association permit foreign students in the U.S. on visas to play in varsity contests?** _____

**In sub-varsity contests?** _____

---

*Residence requirements* seem to bring out the worst in people. A significant percentage of parents seem to have no qualms about falsifying registration papers and other school documents in order to get their children into the schools they prefer. School administrators regularly encounter elaborate charades conducted by people who are determined to fraudulently enroll one or more children in a particular school or district. Although some schools require that incoming transfers provide evidence of legal residence (receipts from landlords, telephone hook-ups, etc.), a personal visit to the address claimed remains the best verification.

There are in most states limited exceptions to residence requirements, especially to accommodate students who are wards of the court, foster children, or residents of group homes. Children of divorced parents are permitted some mobility, but most states place limits on the number of allowable transfers between parental homes.

 *Guardianship* requirements are not identical in all states, but it is safe to say that every state association has established a policy on guardianship. Many define it as a formal legal arrangement. Some (like Washington) specify that "the guardian" is "the adult(s) who has/have had legal custody of the student(s) for a period of at least one year and with whom the student resides."

## *eligibility*

*Turnouts* are practice sessions. Typically, students are required to participate in ten or fifteen turnouts before competing in their first interscholastic contest in a season. Exceptions may be made for those who were involved in playoffs in the previous seasons of competition. This is a safety issue, and it will be strictly enforced by those who have the best interests of the students at heart.

---

**How many turnouts must your students attend before competing in a contest?** _____

---

 *Transfers*: this entire subject should be a super red alert! The prudent AD will approach every sports-playing transfer student as a potential source of scandal, forfeits, and deep stress. If the transfer is an outstanding performer, you can be certain that administrators and coaches in competing schools will inquire about the legitimacy of the transfer's residency. (Also expect questions from the adults close to any student whose position is about to be taken by the transfer.)

I strongly recommend that the AD determine the following facts in every case involving a sports-playing transfer. Use this as a checklist:

_____ Up-to-date transcript has been received from previous school through official channels—not hand-delivered.

_____ Transcript shows date student entered ninth grade.

_____ Student has attended less than four years of high school.

_____ Student was attending school in previous semester.

_____ Current grade report indicates that GPA satisfies standards.

_____ Address claimed has been verified by a personal visit.

_____ Place of residence is in the proper attendance area.

*eligibility*

    \_\_\_\_    If student has a guardian, legality of the arrangement has been verified.

    \_\_\_\_    Record includes copy of birth certificate.

After you have worked through this checklist, your final step is to make a telephone call to an administrator at the last school attended by the transfer. Ask, "Is there any reason to regard this as anything other than a legitimate, run-of-the-mill transfer?"

 Never, never, never short-cut these checks. Always wait for the arrival of official transcripts from the transfer's previous school(s). Take all the time you need to verify all information provided by the student and the parents or guardians. Keep in mind that the vast majority of an AD's nightmares are caused by eligibility issues, and most of these issues probably arose because someone was given the benefit of the doubt. The more talented the transfer, the more carefully you must check.

# Emergencies

For the sake of their students, coaches should have an established, practiced procedure for dealing with serious injuries. The future well-being of a seriously injured student may depend on the coach's ability to take necessary action with the greatest possible speed. Appendix 1 of this book describes a sample emergency drill. Read it; have you developed and practiced a similar procedure?

It has long been a common practice for coaches to maintain a file of "emergency cards," which are extremely useful in the event of an accident, injury, team transportation problem, or other unpredictable occurrence. One set of cards can be kept in the team trainer's kit.

 Emergency cards must be signed by a parent or guardian. They must contain the following crucial information:

- insurance coverage
- emergency provider preferred
- hospital preferred
- allergies, medications, and other factors that may affect treatment

# Equipment

An important legal and safety duty of the AD is the inspection of football helmets. Any helmets purchased must be certified by the manufacturer to meet NOCSAE standards; keep records of this on file permanently. Before the beginning of every season, inspect the helmets in use to make sure that there are no weakened or damaged areas prohibited under the standard. Finally, helmets may be used only a stated number of years, so annual inventory checks must be made to identify and eliminate helmets that have reached their "pull date."

Inventories from every head coach should be on file in the AD's office. As sporting goods have risen in price, annual inventories have also increased in importance. This is especially true of "big ticket" items such as wrestling mats, uniforms, and gymnastics equipment.

Be on the alert for "school talk" of athletes having received gifts from shoe companies or from boosters. Accepting a pair of top-of-the-line sneakers can take away a student's amateur standing.

You would be amazed if you knew how many coaches have made presents to their players of game jerseys and other school-bought equipment items. This is not only irresponsible, it is a violation of law. Gifts of "public funds" are illegal in all states. To make certain that this does not occur in your athletic department, be quite clear in explaining to your coaches that they are accountable for the uniforms and equipment that have been provided by the school. This includes material given to the school by boosters clubs.

## Expulsions

See "Suspensions and Expulsions."

## Facilities

Courts have consistently held that there must be regular inspections of the areas in which school sports occur, including facilities for spectators. Once an unsafe condition has been noted, it must immediately be called to the attention of the person responsible for correcting unsafe conditions. The regular inspection routine should include a form for reporting potential hazards.

## *facilities*

Gyms require frequent and regular inspections. Particular attention should be paid to crash pads, bleachers, floor anchors, locker-room light switches, and snap-back basket rims. Watch out for excessive wax, slippery floors, protruding corners, and sharp metal edges.

School fields and courts which are used by non-school groups require extra attention. Before each use, team members should do a quick survey of the area, looking for broken

**Who is most likely to be held responsible for the condition of sports facilities at your school?**

_____

**Who monitors the established inspection routine?**

_____

**Who is responsible for correcting unsafe conditions?**

_____

glass, ankle-twisting holes, sharp bolts on posts, torn wire, and other potential hazards.

Appendix 2 shows a simple checklist for inspections of typical sports facilities.

# Injuries

Many schools arrange to have emergency medical units available at all home football games. Some provide them only for varsity games, which seems odd, since there are usually more sub-varsity contests.

Coaches should be provided with written instructions for dealing with injuries or accidents that occur at "away" contests. The trainer's kit that goes with the team to "away" contests should include copies of all team members' emergency cards (see "Emergencies" above).

Some school districts require the completion of an accident report form whenever there has been an incident involving a physical injury to an athlete, cheerleader, spectator, or other person present at an event.

 You want to see angry? You will if your coaches fail to demonstrate reasonable concern for injured students. For example, any time a student's injury requires transportation by ambulance, be certain that the student is accompanied by a coach, trainer, or chaperone. Common sense requires that concern be demonstrated.

---

**At what events does your school have an emergency medical unit on hand?**

_____

_____

_____

_____

**Under what circumstances must an accident report be filed?**

_____

_____

_____

_____

---

# Insurance

Almost every school has a specific form that students and their parents must complete to establish eligibility to participate in school activities. One important requirement of this form is providing proof of insurance. Although many schools make "school insurance" available, usually at a very reasonable cost to participants, most are satisfied if parents produce evidence that their family has adequate coverage.

 The coach who permits participation by an uninsured student has gone beyond foolishness. If the student is injured, negligence is self-evident. Students who have failed to meet the conditions of participation, including proof of insurance, can be counted on to beg, plead, and argue for some slack—especially at the opening of the season. Coaches must say "No." Period—end of discussion.

 The past two decades have been marked by massive judgments awarded to students who have suffered catastrophic injuries. Few regular insurance policies are adequate to care for those who suffer permanent physical damage while participating in school sports. The National Federation of State High School Associations (11724 N. W. Plaza Circle, Kansas City, MO 64195-0626) offers insurance services, including the National Student Catastrophic Injury Program.

## Legal risks

Beginning in the mid-1970s, sports-related lawsuits became commonplace in public schools. Owing to the extremely high cost of long-term care for those who suffer serious head, neck, or spinal injuries, lawsuits are all but certain to follow such occurrences. Schools can expect to lose these suits if they are found to have been lax in their responsibilities to "warn, inform, and prevent."

For information and guidance regarding potentially harmful practices (dangerous drills, water deprivation, etc.), call on your local sports medicine practitioners. You may be able to have a sports medicine specialist give a seminar for your coaches. Ask coaches to provide written plans for continuing education that warns, informs, and seeks to prevent injuries. The plans may include lectures, demonstrations, posters, and videos.

It is not true that those who turn out for a sport have automatically signified their acceptance of all the many risks inherent in that sport. The courts have consistently held that you can assume only the risks that you are aware of. Further, the individual can only assume "normal" risks, not those created or exacerbated by inadequate supervision or instruction, defective equipment, or other negligence.

It is critical that coaches understand that mere knowledge of the risks among students is not enough. They must understand and appreciate the risks. Thus, the coach should maintain, in the AD's files, a record of his or her frequent and recorded reminders to the students. This documentation will protect the school in the event of a lawsuit.

# Non-discrimination

Twenty-five years ago federal legislation, known as "Title IX" ("title nine"), was enacted to require schools to provide equal opportunity for all students and to forbid discrimination on the basis of gender, race, ethnicity, and other characteristics. The law does not require dollar-for-dollar spending on male and female teams, but it does require that fairness be demonstrated in budgeting and spending, especially in the purchase of equipment essential for safety.

It may seem hard to believe, but there are still some school districts in which Title IX has yet to be fully implemented. There remain a few coaches and administrators who seek to maintain "traditional" advantages for boys in areas such as scheduling, access to facilities, travel, budgeting, and other sports management areas. Good faith and common sense require compromise.

When a question arises over whether males may play on the volleyball team, or females on the wrestling team, consult your state association handbook. Most state associations have long ago dealt with these issues. Courts have generally ruled in favor of "separate but equal" solutions, except in sports where there is no direct counterpart for girls, such as football and wrestling.

Title IX requires that a survey be conducted every three years to be certain that students are being provided with the opportunities to participate in the sports activities they most desire. The AD writes up this survey and has it distributed to all students, then analyzes the returned questionnaires to help determine whether the mix of sports offered should be changed. All the activities need not be interscholastic, and practicality need not be ignored. In addition to surveys, schools should conduct audits of their interscholastic activities programs to determine the extent to which federal and state laws are being enforced. The AD should retain a file of this material to demonstrate compliance with federal requirements.

## Out-of-season activities

This is an area in which, to say the least, the lines have been blurred. Most associations still prescribe starting and ending dates for seasons, but the truth is that coaches have found and exploited so many loopholes that these dates have become all but meaningless. On this subject, coaches and the state are often in opposition: the state attempts to encourage students to engage in several sports, but many coaches push students to "make a choice," to specialize.

A common tactic used by school coaches to skirt the rules is to arrange for "proxies" (AAU, city recreation departments, Boys and Girls Clubs, etc.) to sponsor out-of-season activities.

Summer camps have become major revenue producers for colleges and individuals. They also provide opportunities for recruiters to observe and make early contact with high school students. There is considerable difference of opinion among coaches and athletic administrators on the value of such camps for the majority of students. In many states, these summer camps fall outside the jurisdiction of the state association.

In 1997 the *Seattle Times* referred to football as "the fastest-growing spring sport." Among the schools engaging in questionable spring football was at least one that not only had more days of practice than the University of Washington Huskies, it had more days of contact. While state associations must wrestle with this problem, it is the AD who must be concerned about safety issues like the following:

- Who performs equipment and facility inspections for out-of-season activities?
- Who enforces school policies regarding insurance?
- Are physical exams required?
- Who is responsible for compliance with eligibility requirements?
- Whose uniforms and equipment are being used?
- Who is responsible for emergency services?

 It is becoming more necessary for ADs to be on the lookout for exploitation of student-athletes. Although fewer than 2 percent of high school athletes receive significant financial aid (let alone "full rides") on completion of high school, these "blue-chippers" require the services of average athletes to serve as supporting casts when they showcase their talents on national and international tours, in tournaments, "team camps," and "sports schools." This may mean that kids are being pressured to devote time, money and energy, and give up vacations and other interests, to a single activity. They may be pressured to deprive themselves of opportunities to more fully experience other school and outside activities, in order to promote a small number of scholarship candidates — or, worse, to promote the selfish interests of an ambitious coach.

## Paperwork

The following checklist notes documents that the AD should have, on file and at hand, regardless of whether the state association or local school district requires them.

\_\_\_\_\_    Eligibility lists

\_\_\_\_\_    Emergency plans

\_\_\_\_\_    Facilities inspection schedules and records

\_\_\_\_\_    Inventories of equipment and uniforms

\_\_\_\_\_    Playoff registration forms

\_\_\_\_\_    Weight loss certificates (wrestling)

_____ Up-to-date record of coaches' First Aid/CPR certifications

_____ Contest schedules for all teams, in all sports

_____ Current team rosters

_____ Transportation schedules

_____ Injury/accident reports

_____ School policies on substance abuse, attendance, academic eligibility, etc.

_____ Parental permission forms signed for activities and trips

## Parental permission

Many schools require the completion of a "clearance procedure" which includes, at the very least: insurance; the payment of fees for specific sports and/or for membership in the local students' association; proof of a recent physical exam; and a parent's or guardian's signature on an "Official Permission to Participate" form. The best forms are those that both inform the parents/guardians in clear, unambiguous language about "clearance" requirements, and provide evidence that students have parental permission to participate.

 If a coach or AD has reason to suspect that someone other than a parent or guardian has signed the Parental Permission form, it is advisable to seek confirmation with a letter or phone call. Experienced coaches know that a student who has failed to satisfy participation requirements may take foolish risks in order to join in "tryouts." Parental permission is not just a formality and must be treated as a non-negotiable element in the clearance process.

## Parents

Parents of student-athletes have rights. They deserve that:

- Their children's coaches will be professionals who know what they're doing.
- Their children will be treated with respect.
- Safety will always be a primary concern of coaches.
- Coaches will be considerate of family life.
- Coaches will model honorable behavior.
- Coaches will listen to them courteously and respectfully.

Parents do not have the right to interfere in the coach's efforts to create a team, by sowing seeds of discontent because their own ambitions for their children are not being realized. When parents who are consumed by self-interest begin to harass a coach, the AD must make clear his or her opposition to such tactics. One possible strategy is to refuse to listen to complainers until the parents have had a face-to-face discussion with the affected coach.

The AD cannot be neutral when parents attempt to interfere in a coach's conduct of a school sports program. Generally speaking, it is a mistake for an AD to provide a sounding board for complaints against a coach from those who have not confronted the coach with their concerns.

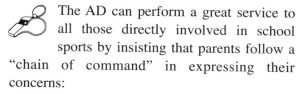 The AD can perform a great service to all those directly involved in school sports by insisting that parents follow a "chain of command" in expressing their concerns:

1.  individual coach
2.  head coach
3.  athletic director

4, principal
5, superintendent
6, school board

The AD should never agree to cooperate in keeping secret the complaints of parents. There will be occasions when the AD is approached by parents who "don't want Bill (the coach) to know that I came to you."

 When a student is disciplined by a coach (sent from practice, suspended, or "kicked off"), it is very important to advise the student's parent or guardian. The coach will need to communicate concerns and outline a plan for resolving the student's problem.

Through a boosters club, the AD and other school officials can provide educational information to parents and fans regarding their roles in the school sports programs. For example, it should be made clear that coaches alone are responsible for making decisions about squad selection and playing time.

If there is no boosters club, the AD can schedule informational meetings just before the start of the various seasons. During the season, some coaches or ADs produce a monthly newsletter for players, parents, and fans.

## Physical exams

There is no greater demonstration of concern for the welfare of participants than the widespread requirement that participants, prior to the first practice session in any sport, be thoroughly examined by a medical authority licensed to perform physicals. (This may be an M.D., Doctor of Osteopathy, Doctor of Naturopathy, Nurse Practitioner, Physician Assistant, or some other designated practitioner; state and local rules list approved medical authorities.) Schools usually have their own forms for the examiner to fill out; on this form the examiner writes a statement as to the fitness of the student to participate in the designated sport, and signs it.

In some areas, especially where medical practitioners are not numerous, school districts may be able to arrange for examiners to provide a "group physical." There will almost certainly be a fee for this service, and the examiners may require that the exams be held somewhere else than a gym.

Read your state and local rules to determine whether a physical exam in the summer can satisfy the requirements of fall, winter, and spring sports. Do not take it for granted that a physical exam for football will satisfy requirements for participation in track and field.

It's a good idea to keep on file, for several years, the physical exam forms collected by the athletic department. If the AD suspects forgery on some document, the files can provide signatures for comparison.

## Recruiting

There certainly have been—and will continue to be—efforts by coaches to encourage or persuade gifted athletes to switch schools. The rules are easy to understand, but there will always be some who are willing to cheat or lie. In general, coaches (or other school representatives) are prohibited from offering any inducement, of any kind, to encourage or facilitate the transfer of a student for athletic purposes.

Because all the participants in illegal recruiting are attempting to "get around the rules," being able to prove that recruiting has occurred is usually extremely difficult. ADs need to convince coaches that they may "get away" with a recruiting violation, but they'll lose stature with their peers and supervisors.

## Referees, officials, and umpires

As the AD, it is likely that you are responsible for securing the services of officials for every "home" event. This is not the daunting task it once was, thanks to the work of assigning secretaries in the various officials' organizations. Call your state association for a list of officials' organizations and their assigning secretaries.

Coaches should be involved in the process of obtaining and scheduling officials. In some leagues, there may be limited opportunities to rate, rank, or "blackball" officials, and the AD will need to consult with affected coaches.

**Fill in the telephone numbers of the officials' organization(s) you will need to contact.**

_____

_____

_____

_____

_____

_____

_____

The home school is always responsible for hosting game officials and for ensuring their safety. Protecting officials from harassment and harm is a primary responsibility of school officials, including coaches. A secure dressing area for officials is a must.

# Scheduling

Many leagues (or conferences) provide master schedules and leave to the ADs the responsibility of "filling in" the non-league dates with opponents of their choice.

Coaches should always be given the opportunity to express their preferences in scheduling, especially when they are expected to have practices and/or contests during vacation periods.

The AD will be scheduling for several teams in each sport (frosh, soph, jayvee, and varsity) in as many as twenty sports. The chances for embarrassing errors and conflicts multiply in seasons where postponements are not uncommon, as in spring. In order to avoid scheduling disasters (for example, two competing teams on buses that pass on the freeway, going in opposite directions), there are two steps that a prudent AD will take:

- Send a one-page "contract" to each opponent, stating all the contests agreed to, in all sports, in a particular season.
- Mail "reminder" postcards two weeks in advance of each scheduled contest, especially in the spring.

*scheduling*

In most states, prior approval must be obtained from the state association by teams wishing to compete against out-of-state or foreign teams.

Assume nothing! Check everything! For every AD who is "on top of things," well organized and responsible, there is another who is not. The latter can make life all too interesting for the former! The prudent AD relies on an ounce of prevention by sending contracts and reminders to colleagues.

## Specific sports

There are contest limitations in all sports, as well as regulations on the frequency with which individuals and teams may compete. To ascertain the rules specific to each sport, check state association handbooks. In addition, there are minimum workout requirements for each sport.

## Sportsmanship

Sportsmanship is a lot like the weather. Everybody talks about it, but few do anything meaningful about it. Although everybody gives lip service to the concept of honorable conduct, few coaches make it a priority, carefully devising drills, planning lessons, maintaining statistics, or developing reward systems. Most of the time, when you hear sportsmanship being discussed, it's because some youngster is being chided for misbehaving in public.

One way to call public attention to the subject is to have the athletic department sponsor a schoolwide essay contest: "Good Sportsmanship in the Twenty-first Century." Permit no negatives: writers are to tell what it is, not what it isn't. Copy the best essays for broad distribution in the community, and discuss them with student-athletes.

Ask coaches to contribute examples of successful lessons in sportsmanship that they have observed or used. Compile them into a handout called "How to Teach Sportsmanship." You may collect some worthwhile tips, and you will definitely heighten awareness that good sportsmanship must be taught, not just assumed.

Enlist the aid of boosters in observing student-athletes to catch them in acts of good sportsmanship. Reward the acts in some imaginative way.

 Coaches must be conscious that one coach modeling good sportsmanship is worth fifty who merely talk about it. Whether they intend to or not, coaches provide models whenever they are in the presence of students.

## Substance abuse

An increasing amount of sobering evidence contradicts the traditional notion that playing sports helps prevent substance abuse. Most research seems to indicate that (at least among boys) athletes are more likely than non-athletes to abuse alcohol and experiment with drugs. One explanation of this may be that athletes are likely to be risk-takers. Another contributing factor may be the nation's sports pages, which regularly report the exploits of substance-abusing, media-hyped sports superstars. The bottom line is that is is foolish for any AD or coach to assume that the school's athletes are all "clean."

Your school undoubtedly has a substance abuse policy, and it probably has a special policy that applies to those who represent the school and community as members of teams. The policy has probably been printed and distributed to all team candidates. This is only the beginning! The policy should also be printed in school and community newspapers. It should be mailed to parents and guardians of student-athletes, and all should be invited to meetings at which school personnel thoroughly explain the school district's policies.

The policy must be vigorously monitored and vigorously enforced. It is vitally important that students (as well as adults in the community) are able to see that enforcement is consistent, fair, even-handed, and unflinching. Public perception will determine how successful your substance abuse policy will be.

Remember that peer pressure is a major factor in a youth's decision to use or avoid illegal substances. If athletes know they will be suspended from competition if they are found drinking or using drugs, the disapproval of their deserted teammates may be something they want to avoid more than the disapproval of adults.

Drug testing, when properly conducted, has been found legal by the U.S. Supreme Court *(Vernonia SD v. Acton,* 1995).

 Beware the voices that whine, "Careful! If you actually enforce the rules, you may harm the youth's chances for a scholarship." Institutional failure to hold students accountable for their own actions is a disservice to everyone, but the greatest disservice may be to the gifted athletes who, too often, are taught that "special people" don't have to worry about the rules that "regular people" are expected to follow.

## Supervision

Even though classroom teachers are frequently warned not to leave their rooms unsupervised when students are present, an unfortunate number fail to heed this warning. What's more, many coaches are not teachers and have not even been exposed to these reminders. There may not, then, be a general awareness that supervisors are expected to supervise. Coaches must be in a position to supervise all parts of an area in which an activity is occurring. To illustrate: you can't supervise the field from the coaches' office.

A coach should never leave the site where an activity is occurring. Proper planning and organization will make it unnecessary for coaches to leave their charges unattended.

 Unsupervised locker and shower rooms are accidents waiting to happen. These areas must be regarded as part of the coaches' responsibility to supervise.

Coaches are expected be sufficiently competent that they can identify potentially dangerous activities and take extra precautions to protect their students from harm.

## Support personnel

The services of a great many people are required at games, meets, and matches. Scheduling workers for several hundred events in a nine-month period requires impressive organization. Well-organized ADs use checklists and a scheduling calendar to minimize problems that are common in this aspect of sports management.

Here's a tip: Copy the monthly scheduling calendar and place copies in the hands of all support personnel who are scheduled to work, thereby providing timely reminders.

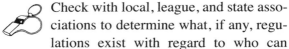 Check with local, league, and state associations to determine what, if any, regulations exist with regard to who can serve as scorekeepers, timers, judges, and other key officials.

## Suspensions and expulsions

There's a rule of thumb: If there's a penalty to pay, there's an opportunity to appeal. ADs need to know, and to inform others, about the possible grounds for appeal, the official procedures to follow, and the deadlines for filing.

Many state associations require that a suspension from the next scheduled contest must occur if a student-athlete is expelled from an interscholastic contest for gross misconduct (fighting, abusive language, flagrant fouling, etc.).

ADs and coaches need to know the school policy regarding suspensions from school. Many schools bar suspended students from being on campus, at any time, during the periods of their suspensions. In general, suspension from school means, at the very least, a suspension from sports.

When discussing appeals with students and their parents or guardians, always use a printed checklist of the appeal procedure as you present the facts and options. Give a copy to all present, then cover each item on the checklist, giving special attention to deadlines. At the close of the conference, ask the student and accompanying adults to sign your copy, indicating that you have provided complete information. The time it takes you to put a checklist together will be very well spent if ugly conversations start—"You didn't tell us that!"

---

**What is your school's policy on participation in sports by students who are suspended or expelled?**

_____

_____

_____

---

# Transportation

The AD or coach should make early contact with the school's transportation department to:

- obtain copies of last year's requests and schedules, and
- inquire about problem areas that need special handling.

The simple act of extending professional courtesy to a colleague will do a lot to ease your relationship with the transportation department.

Be certain to find out what the school district's policy is regarding allowing nonparticipants to ride on team buses or vans.

Some schools use district-owned or rented vans to transport small groups. The AD should find out from school district officials whether the van drivers are required to be specially trained and/or licensed.

Be certain that your coaches know what to do if a bus breaks down or has an accident, or if a student rider cannot be located for the trip home.

Frequently remind all coaches that they are responsible for supervising their students in team buses and vans. Suggest that they probably need to sit in the back of the bus, where they can actually see what's happening!

# Uniforms

Each state association has established rules in many sports to standardize colors, lettering, and numbering of uniforms. Check your rule book before you order!

Theft of school sports equipment is a nation-wide problem. The department needs a secure storage area for inventoried uniforms and gear.

# Warnings

See the section above on "Legal risks" for the importance of warning participants about risks and hazards associated with their activity.

# Appendix 1
# Sample Emergency Drill

In the event of a serious injury, there are important tasks that must be immediately carried out. (Two people are assigned to each task, so that a "sub" will be available if the primary person responsible is absent.)

## The following assignments are for the month of: *December*

1.  *First Aid Provider* (coach, trainer) determines injury to require Emergency Aid, directs Designated Caller to notify emergency provider.
    a. Head Coach Dick King
    b. Jayvee Coach Bill Howell

2.  *Designated Caller*—Calls Emergency Services provider, using number posted next to (or on) designated "emergency phone".
    a. Duffy Dyer
    b. Pete Bushong
    "This is Duffy Dyer. I am calling from

East Plato High School. This is an emergency. A student has been injured and requires immediate assistance. There will be guides posted at the entrances to the parking lot on 10th and Court, to assist the Aid Car in finding the scene." (Stay on phone, to answer questions.)

3.     *Guides*—Sprint for designated positions and watch for the Emergency Vehicle(s). Direct it/them to the access nearest the injured person/people.

    a. Dale McIntyre

    b. David Lopez

    c. Tonio Johnson

    d. Corky Fenton

*Note*: Guides will need to be instructed to attract the attention of Aid Car drivers, perhaps by waving their arms or waving towels or shirts.

4.     *Door Watchers*—Stand at doors, to provide assistance to Emergency Assistance Personnel.

    a. Don Vaughn

    b. Frank Armijo

5. ***Emergency Supplies Bearer***—At the direction of the First Aid Provider (see #1), brings needed equipment to site of injury. This equipment may be First Aid Kit, blankets, sandbags, ice, etc. Bearer must know, in advance, where Emergency Supplies are kept.

a. Bill Demory

b. Ernest Sanders

Now—be sure to have "emergency drills at least once every two weeks, in order to ensure that your system works to ensure the best possible emergency response.

# Appendix 2
# Sample Inspection Record

1.  *Gymnasium* was inspected on
    _____

    \_\_  Wall pads under baskets
    \_\_  Backboards and rims
    \_\_  Padding on Scorer's Table
    \_\_  Floor inserts (for standards)
    \_\_  Bleachers

    Recommended actions: _____
    _____

2.  *Locker Rooms* were inspected on
    _____

    \_\_  Locker handles
    \_\_  Benches
    \_\_  Switchplates
    \_\_  Shower room floor
    \_\_  Shower fixtures
    \_\_  Cleaning

    Recommended actions: _____
    _____

## *sample inspection record*

3. ***Tennis Courts*** were inspected on
   _____

   __ Hardware on posts
   __ Cables, nets
   __ Wire on backstops
   __ Surface
   __ Cleaning

   Recommended actions: _____
   _____

4. ***Football/Soccer Field*** was inspected on
   _____

   __ Goalposts (anchors, padding)
   __ Soccer goals
   __ Surface (for holes, broken glass, etc.)
   __ Sprinkler heads
   __ Sideline obstructions
   __ Bleachers
   __ Restrooms
   __ Press Box
   __ Concession stand(s)

   Recommended actions: _____
   _____

5. ***Baseball and Softball Fields*** were inspected on _____

___ Home plate

___ Pitcher's rubber

___ Outfield (for holes, broken glass, etc.)

___ Infield surface

___ Base anchors/inserts

___ Backstop

___ Bleachers

___ Dugouts

___ Concession stand(s)

Recommended actions: _____

_____

Similar inspection must be made for ***Wrestling, Volleyball, Track and Field, Gymnastics***(!) and other sports. These can be added to your Inspection Record. The inspections are not a burden when spread over several days and performed no more often than once a month.

# About the Author

Dick King has been directly involved in interscholastic sports for forty-five years as a coach, athletic director, teacher, consultant, and clinician. He has taught graduate courses for coaches and athletic directors. A successful basketball coach for thirty-five years, he also enjoyed directing high school and community college teams in football, baseball, and track and field. His profession took him to Iowa, Missouri, Arizona and Washington. He is past president of the Washington Secondary Schools Athletic Administrators Association. A popular banquet speaker, Dick King was a clinician for Medalist Sports Industries, a committeeman for the National Association of Basketball Coaches, and a presenter for the National Sports Promotion Association. He is the author of *The Reality-based Classroom* and *The Courage to Coach,* and coauthor of *The Professionally Responsible Athletic Director.*

# Additional notes:

# Additional notes:

_____

_____

_____

_____

_____

_____

_____

_____

_____

_____

_____

_____

_____

_____

# Additional notes:

# Additional notes:

_____

_____

_____

_____

_____

_____

_____

_____

_____

_____

_____

_____

_____

_____

_____

_____

# Additional notes:

# Additional notes:

_____

_____

_____

_____

_____

_____

_____

_____

_____

_____

_____

_____

_____

_____

_____

_____

To order additional copies of

# The Pocket Athletic Director

Book: $14.95    Shipping/Handling: $3.50

Contact: ***BookPartners, Inc.***
P.O. Box 922
Wilsonville, OR 97070

E-mail:  bpbooks@teleport.com
Fax:  503-682-8684
Phone:  503-682-9821
Order:  1-800-895-7323